MORE WINDS

MORE WINDS

A Second Collection of Poems

Carol H. Ehrlich

with cover painting by
Willem A. Wils

MORE WINDS
A SECOND COLLECTION OF POEMS

iUniverse books may be ordered through booksellers or by contacting:

iUniverse
1663 Liberty Drive
Bloomington, IN 47403
www.iuniverse.com
1-800-Authors (1-800-288-4677)

ISBN: 978-1-5320-9411-8 (sc)
ISBN: 978-1-5320-9412-5 (e)

Print information available on the last page.

iUniverse rev. date: 01/30/2020

DEDICATION

More Winds is dedicated to my family–that from which I came, and that which I helped produce. They are my stream of life.

Contents

ACKNOWLEDGEMENTS

What a blessing to have had the generosity of so many people during the course of my writing!

At the beginning, Lew Sarett, comes to mind. He was one of my professors and a legend at Northwestern University; he opened the world of free verse to me, including the beautiful and simple writings of Carl Sandburg, his friend. They started me on this journey. (Other well-known poets, too many to list, contributed, so I thank them all.) The germ was planted.

I've been lucky to work since then with three writers' groups during different periods in my life—the Aspen Writers in Aspen, Colorado, the Island Writers' on Sanibel Island, Florida, and the Denver chapter of American Penwomen in Denver, Colorado. Several individuals from these groups made particularly significant contributions to my thinking—Karen Chamberlain, Bruce Berger, Betty Anholt, Jean Jensen, Jack Chappell, Don and Eleanor Brown, Dick Jacker, Di Saggau, Andrea Antico, Diane Chambers, Kelly Ann Compton, Atlanta Sheridan, Kay Taylor, Cathy Wield, and Ruthy Wexler. Talented and accomplished writers are among them.

In recent years I've followed and been inspired by the work of Rosemerry Wahtola Trommer, a unique and prolific poet who commands enormous respect in Colorado literary circles. I love and wish her work were mine!!

I would be seriously remiss if I neglected to thank Henry Claman, M.D., a wonderful Renaissance man, who pushed me to submit my work to *Human Touch*, a literary and arts journal. Henry's belief in my writing made a huge difference in my life, prompting a move from private and personal into the broader world cum recognition, criticism and reward. He is gone now, but I shall always remember him for his caring and persistence—and, of course, for his own inimitable literary style.

Thanks to Bill Wils, such a talented watercolorist! His sailboat graces the covers of this and my last volume. So lucky to have had such a dear, generous friend......

The ultimate acknowledgements must begin with Max, my husband of almost 70 years, who gave love and encouragement unstintingly to me throughout those years. There is no possible substitute for that gift, no adequate thank you. I was so blessed! Then Rick, Gloria and Peter, our children, now grown, seasoned and thoughtful, have cheered me on despite times when they were dealing with their own challenges and may have wished I'd give it a rest. JoAnn and Laura, both spouse/in-laws, contributed their ideas and their caring. Knowing, too, that my grandchildren read my work has spurred me on. How richly I've been supported all this time! Saying "thank you" is simply not enough. I can only hope all of these good people receive this kind of support in their own ventures.

So after all that, it is time to lay it out for you. Good, good, good!

INTRODUCTION

More Winds follows my earlier collection, Winds in My Sails, adding recent work without altering the impetus for the writing....then or now. Many strands of living, the "winds" in these books, have affected me in simple and complex ways. You can see them thread through the writing if you compare the 2005 Introduction with my current remarks that follow.

Introduction, 2005, WINDS IN MY SAILS

After writing factual and objective material most of my adult life, poetry has become a late-life dessert. It offers a drastically different challenge, always more intimate, more revealing and therefore more courageous, and certainly more fun. The charge in both is truth; however poems can couch that truth in creative, sometimes playful language.

It seemed an indulgence initially, turning away from carefully organized, objective (i.e. sterile) writing whose only task is to communicate certain information clearly and completely, to work with a poem. I have found great pleasure in allowing my feelings to enter, in exploring the richness of the English language to express my messages in unexpected and creative ways. It has been liberating to treat as valid any of my experiences and sensory knowings for inclusion in what I write, and to say it in whatever way comes to me.

With joy I offer to my family and other readers this variety of poems. They cover everyday and exceptional material, sad and humorous, profound and light-hearted. In capricious currents, feelings and ideas have come to me which called to be committed to paper. The resulting poems reveal the many winds that have affected my sails. I hope you will find in some of them something that will speak to you. Enjoy!!

More Winds has poured in bursts from inside me. Happenings, places and people in my life in recent years have leaked, streamed, stumbled or sneaked out, as the case may be, calling to be digested and described because they couldn't stay inside. New thoughts, new experiences, new needs prompted this volume's poems, because life continually changes. And—hey—I'm crowding 93 as I write this…so if not now, when?

Several of my poems found voice following Max's death. They were hard. Another group deals with my aging and its effects. Some of these poems are also hard, some funny. Some arose with incidents and idiosyncrasies that compelled expression, often unexpected and sometimes comical. So the contents are varied, as is much that's inside me. I expect that is true with you, too.

My work is divided into two parts: personal introspection and the natural world. Actually many poems bridge both. Where the choice could have gone either way, I simply chose one. (Deliberation seemed a wasted effort. The point was to get the poems out there where they could be read.)

The not-so-hidden purpose of producing More Winds is to leave a part of me in my family's hands for "afterwards." A common need, this, to gift that which means most to the ones we love unreservedly. So to the spirit of Max, my dear departed husband, to my daughter, Gloria, and two sons, Rick and Peter, and their wives, Laura and JoAnn, who give me sustenance every day, to my four grandchildren who never cease to amaze me, and to my *twelve* great-grandchildren who may one day embrace this view of Granny, I offer More Winds. Enjoy, and know me better! To my friends and others who happen onto this work, I hope many parts of it will resonate with you.

NATURAL WORLD

"Live in the sunshine, swim the sea, drink the wild air." — Ralph Waldo Emerson

DOLPHINS

Dolphins play in the bay
like little boys
frolicking in front of me
with no thought of observers,
of duties, of rules,
of conditions—
just the sheer joy of being alive,
doing what dolphins naturally do;
doing what they've always done.

They leap and dive, leap and dive
in hypnotic ballet.
Time holds its breath as they dance.
I watch; in synchrony
my muscles awaken
unbidden.

Then with no warning
the dolphins slide away
through a dent in the water.
Gone. No sign remains

except in me.

Carol H. Ehrlich

MAGNOLIAS

Magnolias are budding.
Small shy nubs steal out
from the end of each branch
when no one is looking.
They swell in time–
big as hen's eggs–
compelled by latent urges
to pose, to be noticed,
to taunt the leafy surround,
almost black in its greenness,
with their pearly-white glamour.
Now we watch; we know
their glory is still to come.
Soon the petals will open,
one by one, seductive, each satin curve
bending in curtsy, enticing,
entreating all to bow
in honor to this Southern Queen.

EQUINE SENTINELS

Two horses stand at the fence like statues.
They neither make sound nor move,
the old bay and the brown mare,
shoulder to shoulder, heads together,
round eyes following as we hike by.
What do they make of us–
our age?
our smiles?
our holding hands?
And then their thoughts, if they have them–
are they shared
in some kind of communion?
Are they like us??

Carol H. Ehrlich

BULL MOOSE

A shocking high voice
bugles "I'm King of the Herd!"
Bull Moose is in rut.

STREAM OF LIFE

Life is like Fish Creek.
How so, you say?

In the spring of the year
water burbles its way out,
glad to be alive,
singing, moving, stretching its banks.

The stream soon flows fast and busy
in its season of fullness.
Run, make noise,
produce, expand. It makes itself known.
Fish leap and jump and search
for who knows what?
Life teems with excitement
that seems to have no end.

But water levels do slowly lower
and Fish Creek finally rests,
peace flowing its calm course,
its summer work a memory.
The wonder of the creek
is there for all to see,
never more beautiful
than in its mature age.
We love you, Fish Creek.
We love you, Life.

Carol H. Ehrlich

FEATHERS

Feathers—yellowy-green feathers, lacy.
That's what I see now
when I squint my eyes at the aspen trees.
Asleep all winter, they finally rouse.
They have this urgent look,
like I feel.
"We must get on," they say; "we must
get through with cold. Enough."

No longer brittle,
branches dry and grey for months
now bend and sway to the kiss
of the breeze.
I stare.
I feel them tease my soul awake.

This feather haze changes the outlook of the yard—
of my spirit.
It can happen. I believe it.

RENEWAL

The trees and I are many decades old–
grey, dry, flake-crusted.
Yet today I see the aspen stretch,
weary of winter.
Branches show greening.
Buds swell from their borders
pregnant with the promise of life
like the Spring in me.

Carol H. Ehrlich

THE LAKE BELOW ME

The glassy blue of the lake waits
in innocence, unaware,
not heeding a charcoal cover
stealing in overhead.
I can't warn it. I have no power
to alter nature.

Pox of rain soon dot the surface,
quietly at first.
I watch from my deck.

Coming ever faster, the drops deform the top
of this darkening mirror.
Within minutes they fracture it in frantic shards.
They break the lake
like a pot of water at full boil,
then move in to hide the damage
in sheets of unstoppable rain.
Before my eyes I am losing it—
my idyllic blue jewel below me
in the mountain's once-protective shadow.

I shake my head, sad. I give up,
pull my scarf around me and turn away,
willing myself to wait
for another, a better day.

RAINCLOUD

A wall of raincloud mounts the sky in the north.
edging the horizon's peaks
in black and grey and smoky pink.
It slides noiselessly toward me
like a sheet of liquid
spilling from a gaping inkwell.
It eats the mountaintop as it comes.

I watch without words and hold my breath
expecting the worst.
If losing the sunlight were audible
I would be hearing a dirge.

But even now
in the gloom that envelops me
I know in my bones
that blessed water will soon fall
on our parched earth,
restoring life to all growing things.
I'll breathe in humid air
to ease the dryness in my throat.
Our flowers, our trees, our farms
will wake and stand proud once more.

And tomorrow the sky will clear.
The sun will shine again.

Carol H. Ehrlich

CLIMATE CHANGE

Like old people I have known
the lakes near us shrank, lost their sparkle.
Drought visited…and stayed.
Flats were parched
in wave-shaped lumps
where fish once swam.
Lodge-pole pines thirsted
far too long,
losing their strength
so pine beetles attacked,
boring through their bark,
oozing sticky goo in ugly carbuncles
along the trunks–
a sign of approaching death.

As aging dry skin withers and wrinkles
in the pallor of the very old,
wildflowers wilted and lost color
then bent down
and gave up.

Our wells gave less each day,
jealous of the taking.
Groundwater levels sank
in silent rebuke at waste.

Science has been warning us.
Will we never learn?

EPHEMERAL–

yet seared in my memory–
the luminous gold
of aspen groves
in Colorado's fall–
mountains and hillsides
turned almost overnight
into a radiant blaze
that glows against edges of pine-tree green.

Sadly, it doesn't last.
In weeks, sometimes days,
the leaves blow away in the wind.
Exhausted, drab grey is left—
once golden glory is now
just shades of grey.

But nothing can steal
that jewel-like image. It remains
in the gallery inside my head
to see and relive
any time,
all the long winter long.

Carol H. Ehrlich

WINTER COMING

Gold splotches on the mountain
in morning's growing light
speak words of winter coming
as do the geese in flight.
Snow patches change Mount Baldy
from green to mottled white
and all the signals warn me
to flee southward while I might.

FIRST SNOW

It crept through the cut in the mountain
like Sandburg's little cat feet–
but this time not fog.
It was snow—our first of the season.

From my comfort in the living room
I watched through the sliding glass door
as the film moved in—
grey, then white,
obscuring first the mountains in the rear.
For a time the ridges were edged
as in a fine oil painting, line
on line.
But like spreading milk
that's been spilled
the white soon covered all.
Even the lake below us and
Shadow Mountain on the other side
sucked in the snow.

Snow brings peace, at least sometimes.
Quiet as it falls, it accretes without making a fuss.
Today for example, first there was none,
then in no time my world
was blanketed in softness, in whiteness,
in an implied protection.

But it's not all pleasure, this
first snow of the season.

Carol H. Ehrlich

It changes everything—
from color to black and white,
from sound to global quiet
even in my narrow personal space,
from the warmth and comfort of summer
to the chill and threats of winter.

I welcome the snow because of its beauty,
for the change it brings to my life.
Yet part of me wishes,
in that habit of human nature,
that things could remain unchanged
the way they always were.

FEBRUARY SPARKLES

February sparkles in the sun
outside my window. Snow
fell during the night leaving
a white blanket of glisten
with its promise of fun—
skiing, creating snowmen,
throwing snowballs–
and its profound quiet–
dampening the noise
of traffic and people—
a magic of its own.
February has much to say for itself.

But I prefer to sing in the key of August.

Carol H. Ehrlich

DEEP SOUTH SEASONS

Spring   warm   gentle
   soothing as cream—
   yet tingling.
   New buds   green   birdsong.
Summer   hot   slow   redolent
   damp   cypress   gardenias
   made for hammocks   ceiling fans
   tall icy drinks.
Fall   easy   active
   warm but not too
   dry but not too
   new tomato plants and green oranges
   a second spring turned backwards.
Winter   busy   spangled
   warm   cool   clear   rainy
   each morning a surprise.
   daily indulgence   tangelos
   ruby reds   tomatoes   berries
Deep South seasons circle
   begin   end   begin.
   New life   love
   ever round the bend.

INNER WORLD

"Only from the heart can you touch the sky." — Rumi

PRIMITIVE PLEASURE

Kissed by clean breeze
with fresh smell
that whispers of flowers,
bed linens dry as though ironed
on my wash line at the cabin.

I dip my nose
into lingering scents—
a wanton hungry act
with instant reward.

So easy to fold, so lovely to touch,
these sheets make me wonder
who needs an electric dryer?

Carol H. Ehrlich

ON BECOMING 86 YEARS OLD

I would sing if I could
with voice so pure so clear
only birds would know my song.
They would join in rapture
at life filled with family
with work
with play
with ordinary things like
eating oatmeal and raisins
with my love at my side,
feeling my great-grandbaby's finger
explore my face,
hiking along the shore
of a clear, cold mountain lake–
I catch my breath
at the top of the stairs–
I know all this is still mine to live.

THISTLE

I fell today
tugging out a weed–
a thistle–hardy plant
that didn't want to give up.
I pulled and pulled.
The root said no.
But then the weed got even.
It let go in a burst.
It let me fall backward
down the hill.

At eighty-six, with
osteoporosis and
other fragilities,
I was scared.
I sat up gingerly,
moved everything
I could think of.
Nothing hurt.

I smiled, climbed
back on my feet,
then looked for another
thistle.

Carol H. Ehrlich

THISTLES AGAIN

This year the thistles have returned,
tall as my hip, some of them,
by the time I arrived.
Not only tall, but bearing purple blossoms,
some with white tufts of seed-wings at the top.
They were ready to spread,
and I was ready to do battle, again.

This time I was smart.
Instead of standing below them on the hill
as I did last year to make my stretch easier
I crouched at their side, and pulled.
No more falls down the hill, I promised myself.

This year I was smart, and this year I was lucky.
Rain had softened the earth, and the thistles yielded
without a protest.
Kindly thistles; they knew I was a year older.

HIGH SCHOOL REUNION IN OUR 80'S, IN THE 90'S AN ARITHMETIC JOKE

The first are our ages,
The second the years
we were in high school–
The numbers double
(our age to the years)
and I'm trying to make something of that.
Oh, I know….we're now

twice as smart

twice as beautiful

twice as strong

twice as lucky

twice as skillful

twice as talented

twice as good-hearted

twice as ambitious

twice as much fun

as we ever were in high school.

That's better than the years
to our age
which would be half.
I don't want to be half as…..
Do you?

Carol H. Ehrlich

REMARKABLE STONE

This piece of rock
washed in the river for years
now fits in my palm.
Gleaming surprising colors
it draws my fingers in caress.
Smooth sides like a baby's cheek
are edged in a curve for my thumb
to trace—again and again.
Warming with my warmth
it comforts me.

I stare into space
dreaming impossible dreams.
The silky stone says yes.
It responds between my fingers—
hypnotic
affirming
solid
sure.

KISSES AT THE AIRPORT

I see farewells in all colors–
    a whiff on the cheek,
    hasty, eager to go,
    embarrassed, even,
    some reluctant–
    a duty, maybe—
    a convention to be suffered,
    like the long-obliging husband
    lugging her bags from the car,
    turning, finally,
    a duty goodbye,
    a sigh of relief.
A family, three generations–
    kisses, hugs—repeated,
    insistent, children spilling
    in all directions around Momma,
    Grandma and Grandpa, connecting,
    competing, demanding,
    wringing closeness from
    touch, voice—
    ebullient, irrepressive.
Then the lovers, their silent
    circle enclosed in an
    island of need,
    no more aware of the
    people milling around than
    the plane climbing overhead
    or the guard stopping cars so
    people can cross the road.

Self-contained, they embrace
in a hungry, never-to-end kiss,
arms and bodies pressed close
as one, wanting only no end
to their unity.
And the welcomes too—
varied as buttons in a sewing box.
I watch some travelers as they join
tasting the joy in their eyes, their voices,
when their loved ones arrive.
They rush to kiss, to hold once more
in arms too long empty.
The ties of blood a special case—
Parents to children, young to old—
either way they warm my heart.
My inner eye sees caring, goodness,
so needed in this crazy world.
No performance here.
My eyes well up.
My spirit soars.
Kisses all–
A polyglot of humanity
ties us together.

BEAUTY

We each decide what speaks to us—
color splashed on canvas
or mountainside,
music in the creek's meander
or choir's anthem,
movement in grace from pas de deux
or windblown wheatfield.
Yes, even the art
in words of poets and orators,
the offer of help to those in need
who haven't asked,
in loving a child freely as a true gift from the heart.

You and I might not agree
but in the end they are all one…
beauty.

Carol H. Ehrlich

HITCHED

"Everything in the universe,"
John Muir wrote,
"is hitched to everything else."

His belief floats through me
in an infusion of comfort
and finds a home.

I can be individual, but connected.
I can be by myself, but never solitary.
I am not alone.

I am part of all I touch
while the whole world
sustains me.

JUST WORDS

Invisible, untouchable,
not the thing itself–
just words.

Not real like
the swell in my chest from knowing success–
the ache in my gut that lingers with loss—
the scent of cinnamon and coffee at breakfast–
the blazing gold of fall that takes my breath away.

Words are none of these.
yet with them I can feel the ache and swell,
taste the cinnamon and coffee
see the stunning colors on a mountainside–
know them,
and share them.

Words let me discover my forebears,
pass wisdom to my children.
With them statesmen can know our history
and hope to plot wise pathways.
Words help ideas to form—
abstractions from concrete;
issues to be argued—
no need for fights.

More than that,
words can let out joy, sorrow, anger.
Between us they can change everything.

Valued as precious jewels are
"I'm sorry" "Please" "I love you."

Words are our tools. Our human tools.
They carry our thoughts, our wishes
even create them sometimes—
not always true, not always what we intend,
sometimes cruel, sometimes twisted
and twisting.
Like a hammer, some words bludgeon
and damage.

Then again, they can be gentle,
healing
a soft cocoon to shelter us
a needed breeze for comfort.

A mixed blessing indeed—
sometimes a gift,
sometimes a gift with thorns.
They require care…in the choice,
the delivery, the interpretation.
They are essential.

Don't tell me
they are
just words.

IN NEED OF BOOTS

How far we have come
from my childhood in West Bend
where the police chief was my friend!

He issued my driver's license
when Dad said,
"Boots, she's ready to drive—
Can you take care of her?"

Boots drove me home from the football game
when we learned my boyfriend had been killed
on the road to my school.
I cried on Boots' shoulder.
He cared.

Today
in a large impersonal city
where each man hurries
in a protective cloak
to avoid contact
and conflict,
one man enters the vestibule
of his home
reaches for his wallet
and is gunned down by the police.

Forty-one bullets, nineteen hit their mark.
Much-killed, for no reason
but fear.

Carol H. Ehrlich

How many shots does it take
to stop fear?
A good man, we hear,
this one with the gentle name—
Amadou Diallo—it lilts in soft song—
college-bound,
came with his family to America's shores
to work for a better life.

We gasp. Has it come to this?
The trust, the caring, the hope—
are they long gone?
Can no one remember Boots?

HEARTBREAK 9/11…

gave no warning.
It tore into New York City unannounced.
Perhaps an accident?
I watched TV, holding my breath–
watched the plane crash into the tower.
"No!" I cried out, grasping the arms of my chair.
So sad, so very sad.

Then the second plane,
the second tower.
I stared, unbelieving. My breath stopped.
No accident. The truth–
a horror so strange to me
I found no words.
Only tears.
Sobs.

Terror! Terror right here in my own country!
On our own soil!
My gut knew in that instant
America changed forever…
no words needed.
No more immune to foreign attacks,
no more a peaceful refuge,
we were now part of the warring milieu.
I knew in my bones
life would be forever different.

Stumbling blindly away from the image,
I cried, "No, No!"
but couldn't get away.
The pictures grasped my head, my heart.
I had to escape.
I slid open the sliding door,
stepped out on the deck.

I looked up at Shadow Mountain.
I looked, breathing hard. I tried to make sense.

Then a strange thing happened.
Some easing came over me, a calming.
At that moment, there, the permanence of that mountain
settled on me, like a blanket.

Some things you can count on.
The mountain will remain sure, always there,
dependable, no matter what
we humans do.

I need that reassurance.
Maybe all of us do.

HOW SHALL WE TEACH THE CHILDREN?

How shall we teach the children?
We ask with pain for the knowing
what's out there in this crazy world—
the fraud and deceit, the failure to
care, the bullying, the hate, the killing.

What of the green in the budding tree, you say...
of the strength of the storm,
the fit of the line and sweep of music
even from a single human's soul,
the love in the heart of a parent for a child
and his for a parent?

These hint at life's gifts, a world of
possibilities. There is good to be learned.
Dear babe in my arms, know one day in your bones
what I'm trying so hard to say.

Carol H. Ehrlich

THE MUSIC CALLS

The music calls.
I feel its pull–
not like a flying run down the mountain on skis
still remembered in my aging body
not like a steaming bowl of chili redolent with onion and cheese
on a night that numbs my bones
not like the sweet warm goodness of a well-written book
as I sit propped on pillows in the den–
but a tune, a song in my heart
that migrates to my brain, my ears, my total self.
A song of life, a melody that starts low
and swells in the way of a tide
that holds my breath and never lets go.
The music calls.

FIREPIT MAGNET

They come every weekend
to their cabin,
unload the car,
then head straight to the firepit
in the yard behind.
No dilly-dallying–
purposeful, a driven agenda.
Flames appear within minutes.

Like a magnet
they hold the group in a circle
staring into the blaze
'til almost morning.

What happens inside these people
as they gaze for hours?
Are there dreams in their eyes,
in their hearts?

Do they see what might have been
but never came?
Do they revise their lives in the
flicker and flame
and become what they once wished?

Or are they simply firebugs?

Carol H. Ehrlich

MUSCLE MEMORY

The World Cup, the Olympics
grab my eyes, my heart.
Watching the slalom, the downhill races,
expert skiers in their prime,
I cannot stop my viscera,
my muscle memory.
My quads tighten,
my knees piston up and down
in subliminal action.
I feel the racers' turns
as they course downhill.
Exhilaration fuels my senses
remembering the wind in my face
the beat of the challenge
the biting cold of the air
my racing heart
at the top of the black runs—
the expert ones that scared me.

MOTHER

She lives in my memory clear as
the ring of a tuning fork,
eyes soft and loving, willing to help
when our babies were new;
always there for a question.
She turned worry into comfort.

My memory of her seemed lost for many years.
Now, she is there once more–dreams at night,
impulse in the day to call her on the phone,
desire to let my children know her as I did.

> You can't remember her laugh, how she sang clear liquid soprano
> in the choir, how her black hair flashed blue in the sunlight. How she almost ran
> through the store when shopping, so we were out of breath trying
> to keep up. How she relished a cookie every night, and a good joke.
> How pretty she was, how lovely her bearing.

I knew it was time when she left us. Yet it was hard.
These memories help.
They lie warm and sweet
like a satin blessing in my breast.

Carol H. Ehrlich

MY THREE KIDS

Bright, varied as snowflakes, a challenge to raise—
Rich with talent
barely hidden in childhood
by behaviors born of being
too eager,
too determined,
too impatient
to be social animals.
I knew, but it took some years;
years when I sometimes had to laugh,
or take a deep breath,
sometimes when I despaired.

Memories—they flood my mind–
Gloria finding the miracle of scissors
As she played with her hair;
Peter straddling the ridgepole
of a neighbor's house
at the tender age of six;
Rick working out math theorems on torn envelopes,
any scrap of paper,
when he should have been doing his chores.

And, yes, they had chores—all three.
Old-fashioned, maybe,
but part of the '50s
like peanut butter and jelly.
They and their friends all had chores—
Doing the dishes, (hot water, basin, dishcloth-style)

emptying the trash,
making their beds,
picking up toys—it was
part of life where we lived.

Now adults, they are parents
and grandparents too,
finding their own uncharted paths
as the models, the caregivers,
and their roles a bigger challenge
because of me.
I'm the aging now-great-grandparent
they circle 'round, helping and loving,
warming my heart…

And they don't expect me to pick up the toys!

Carol H. Ehrlich

WHO I AM

Part of me lives alone.
I have shared much with others—
    my children growing up
    my close friends from my youth
    colleagues in my daily work
    neighbors who live nearby
    and especially
    my life-mate–
yet what they know is but a portion
of this person inside.

Who I am formed early, shaped
by mother, father, sister, brother,
then by my children, by parenting–
by a widening circle
of chance encounters
of bondings.

Who I am grows
as I live each new day.
Who I am informs me
how I connect to the world.
Who I am guides me
when I act, when I react.
You may know me, or think you do
but can you always predict
my course, my response?

Who among us has not been surprised,
maybe shocked,
by someone we thought we knew.

You cannot fully know the core self
that inhabits a person,
Internal and complex—
      too broad
      too deep
      too long a story
      to share.

And sometimes we ourselves are surprised!

Carol H. Ehrlich

NEWBORN

His warm moist skin
is smooth under my finger.
I trace the tender curve of his cheek
and purse of his lips
and the moving arch of his arms.
His fingers close around mine
in trust
in seeking human touch.

I would hold in my heart
the wonder of this newborn babe
before his sweet breath and smile
are changed by the real grown-up world

and never forget.

CONTENT?

She seemed content,
rarely crying
as babies do when in need.
She watched,
eyes sometimes wide
sometimes barely open,
always taking it in,
quiet, seemingly untroubled
by noise, by hunger, by wetness—
restless at times, her benign signal.

She absorbed our world,
digested it,
dealt with it—
a pattern that stuck as she grew.
And competence unfolded.
She could handle anything.

I watch proudly
yet wonder what's inside.
What makes her restless now?
At times talkative,
she closes up like a zipper
when I ask.

I wish she would let me in.
No life goes on without problems.
Even hers.
How can I help when I don't know?

UNFINISHED

"Here I am, 75,
and still unfinished,"
you said with a wry look on your face.

"That's okay," I nodded.

"I'm 90, and I too
am still unfinished."

"You and I have worlds to find
people to know
ideas to hear
sights to see
life to live."

"Let's be wide-eyed
'til the day we die."

Carol H. Ehrlich

REALITY

That woman in the reflecting glass
looks back at me…
I stare, and know
without a doubt
each year in my long life
is right there, in my face.

Why didn't I hide
maybe every other year
or every third?

But no. I couldn't stand
to miss anything.

I can't lie. I can't pretend.
    You can read me like the cross-cut
    of the trunk of a tree—
    count the rings
    and know its life.
I have rings,
outside and inside.

Some thread my face—
all over my face.
Every last year is there.
My spirit and will
would deny the years

but the evidence is there.
There in my face.

When he looks at me
does he think of Botox
or someone half my age?

I do hope he has his own mirror!

Carol H. Ehrlich

MY GIFT FOR YOU

My hand outstretched, open,
not holding back
not wanting in return—
my gift:
not the laugh or the sigh we share
but the swell in my chest that follows,
not the sun with its light
but the warmth of my heart,
not the moon in its phases
but my steady alwaysness
you can count on
like the dear mountains
that surround us.
Know this—
I will be there for you even
when I can no longer tell you.

LOVE

Love sometimes lives through quarrels,
fatigue, or too little time.
      though too often
      they fray it at the corners,
      then shatter its core.
With age, surviving love
glows with beauty and strength
like an ancient oak against the setting sun.
      Moments of quarrel, fatigue, neglect,
      become fading static
      while the music grows.
The song swells,
resonates with our lives,
nourishing, sustaining us.

Love transcends the noise.

Carol H. Ehrlich

ORDINARY

Just when I thought
we were too old for romance,
for the old fun that used to
tingle my spine and
tickle my innards—
just when I sighed,
settling, I guess, for a flat plate
of ordinary
for the rest of our days—
just then
I saw your smile,
felt your hand reach my shoulder,
touch my neck
in your old way of knowing.

In a transforming moment
the magic returned—
not the same,
but it tasted so sweet.
A slow-moving lightning
radiated through me.

Oh my...
a new, seasoned world began.

FRIEND

Saying hello the first time
was the sun shining.

Saying hello when we were old friends
was the comfort of the mid-day sun.

Saying goodbye when you left forever
was the sunset. Darkness engulfed me.

But every night
in the mountains
as the alpenglow follows the sunset
I know you haven't gone.
You are with me always.

Carol H. Ehrlich

AFTER THE FUNERAL

So busy
projects to complete
clothes to bundle for Goodwill
papers to digest
forms to fill out—to file–
calls to make
lists to check
friends to contact
visitors to receive
food to buy.
Go go go go
Do do do.
Smile at my neighbor
as I go in and out.
I'm fine.

Dinner's over.
Dark has fallen.
Silence reigns.
It slams my chest
with a strange weight.
My muscles drag
without aim.
My mind can't focus.
I don't smile.
There's no one here.

ALONE

Alone is a lie.
Like slogans and songs
with a one-size story
it is a fake.
No one—nothing—is alone.

Even in my home—
for so many years humming with family,
friends and partner
and now empty of all—
memories remain
nourish me
hold my hand in saving embrace.

Carol H. Ehrlich

SOLITUDE–THOUGHTS OF A NEW WIDOW

Solitude envelops me
like a warm blanket.
Quiet,
strange, unaccustomed,
but I find, a welcome friend.

It makes room for
memories and feelings
that rest and leave comfort
in the echoes of my heart.

ENDLESS JACKSON POLLACK

As I lie in bed at the end of the day thoughts scramble
like children bursting out in all directions
through the school door when the closing bell rings—
no order, no peace, no resolution—
a splatter painting
that flies too fast, too impatient in the race
too scattered to be seen
to be heard
to be dealt with.

I want quiet, a blank slate,
a calm white canvas
so my body will relax and rest will come.
I try to tame the chase; catch one thought and tie it down—
reduce the clamor one piece at a time
so sleep will come.
I want to control my muse
but the party inside has a mind of its own.
It will carry on 'til dawn
despite all my efforts.
It's a losing battle.

Good morning, I guess.

Carol H. Ehrlich

LADY IN #6*

In flat number 6 on a London street
Alice Herz Sommer practiced the piano
three hours a day
even at 109 years of age,
even after imprisonment by the Nazis
for years in Thieresenstadt.

She smiled as she spoke,
"I have no space or time for pessimism or hate."

Oldest Holocaust survivor,
oldest classical pianist,
a beam of light in a dust-filled world,
she admonished, "Don't stand there and cry."
"Understand. Life is beautiful. I have so much
to learn and enjoy."

Like yeast-leavened, expanding dough,
her image fills me, inflates me,
makes me work to understand.
I breathe in the joy
that radiates from her person
and know that anything is possible.

• *Title taken from an Academy Award Short Documentary about Herz-Somers at age 109.*

CORE

They have spoken to me of Venezuelas
of Chilis and of Paraguays.
I have no idea of what they are saying.
I know only the skin of the earth
And I know it is without a name. Pablo Neruda

We are all of the same heart
       grit
       will;
we know the same needs
       desires
       dreams.
We are bound in the human condition.

This consummate garden of life
grows songs to sing
structures to build
children to teach–
a profusion of flowers
in every color.

But like tectonic plates that girdle the earth
shift under pressure
we can quake under stress.
Fears, ignorance, sensing threat
can destroy the spirit,
replace good with evil.

Carol H. Ehrlich

Can we find wisdom
to forge the way,
peace to ease the pressure,
strength to keep the bond?

BECOMING NIRVANA

I'll build my own small world—
a nest, a haven,
a covey peopled by ones I love
and who love me—
where help and caring are the substance
and music the seasoning of the stew.
My world would shine bright
and like daylight that ends the night
would change our war into peace.

Carol H. Ehrlich

ON WAITING FOR MY 12TH GREAT-GRANDCHILD

You'd think eleven would be enough—
each one different
each one special.
Three girls; eight boys…
each unique in gifts, in cautions,
all facing a world of challenge.
Eleven is a handful. A heartful.

And now I await Number 12–
(an even dozen)
gender unknown, at least by me;
resemblance to the family,
innate nature, personality,
responsiveness,
talents—
all so far hidden–
unknown quantities,
yet a babe I love already.

Why, you say?
This unknown bundle
brings mystery, new and old.
Myriad gene strains, even mine,
bring possibility–
possibility, the magic of dreams and wishes.
possibility, the power that moves the world.
How could I not love that babe?

TEARS

Jewel-like, they slip out shiny, wet,
easy, salted with human essence,
free to carry the burdens of
sorrow and pain
outward
where they can breathe
and harm no more.

The soil from which they come,
no longer leaden
with its load of feeling,
can regroup, restore,
come new again with hope.

"I don't cry easily," Margo said.
How sad.
Without tears
the lump in her throat remains an ache
that lingers long,
that holds her life hostage.

I would give her the gift of tears
if I could.

Carol H. Ehrlich

TIME WAS

Time was
when I couldn't stop thinking,
day and night–
solve problems, design pathways,
ponder theories, plan strategies,
figure people out–
intellectual overload
all the time.
"Don't you ever give your brain a rest?"
my young son needled.

Today, at ninety-two, I sit on the deck,
look at the lake and mountain beyond,
hear the hummingbirds at my side,
the motor boats below–
the breeze moves my windchimes,
caresses my cheek,
a perfume of pansies and tomato plants
fills the air—

I hear, I see, I feel it all
in my tissues–
no intellect needed.
Tensions are gone.
I am strangely complete.

CHANGE

My knees know the meaning of decrepitude.
My mind dithers with strands not remembered,
not understood.
My face wears crags and leather,
not the satin glow of youth
back when he eyed me with desire
and we blossomed in the joining.

Impatience to see, to do, to know
that drove my waking hours
that sparkled my eyes
and bubbled smiles from eager lips,
his and mine,
is gentled now.

The knowing has become wider, deeper.
Patience settles my brow and being.
Solitude among a crowd
gives me time to understand
that grains of sand shift and change
in the winds—and so will I.
I sigh,
then shrug.

These are the rewards of living.
They are mine, and I will celebrate!

Carol H. Ehrlich

IT'S LIFE

It's time I learn to live with
a scratchy voice, wrinkles, thinning hair,
working hard to get up and down,
(an elevated toilet seat, for heaven's sake!)
forgetting where I put the checkbook
and what I had for dinner last night.

It's time I accept that necessary nap,
the help from my neighbor to open a jar,
a ride to the book club meeting that is held nearby,
but up a flight of stairs,
passage through a doorway held open by a stranger.

So many things.

It's time to look all that in the face
and say, "OK, my dear!"
"It's life!"

THE TASK

Make a list. Again.
Capture those fragments of thought.
Watch them sift lightly
through the fog
settle for moments…
then blow away.

Work hard.
Woo them back.

Hang onto life.

Carol H. Ehrlich

THE BACK NINE

I travel the back nine
in a reverie,
absorbed in the sweet reward
of nearing completion,
all the time sorry to see the game end,
weighed down by the weary knowing
of shots hit wrong—
misjudged and just plain missed—
yet buoyed by the feeling still in my muscles of
playing well when sometimes I did.

I'd like to play it over,
make the errors disappear,
feel the good shots
once more ring true.
I'd like to wage it like a champion
and wear the triumph in my bones.

The truth is plain, however—
like a concert just over in a crowded hall,
like cycles of nature that never halt,
like the path of the sun,
the history is written.
It is what it is.

Do-overs are not an option.

IT IS TIME

Our wholeness stands luminous
against life's curtain of noise…
No more of transient changes
of trappings taken on, of conflicts,
of confusion, of decisions.

With each goodbye, each flower's embrace,
each easing of pain, each love expressed,
we strip away, and like a single red rose
or a Puccini aria in a now empty hall—
become essence, ourselves,
whole and ready
at peace in the moment
for whatever lies ahead.

AFTERWORD

Some of my poems in <u>More Winds</u> have appeared in prior publications. They include:

It Is Time	Winds in My Sails, 2005
Friend	Winds in My Sails, 2005
Mountain Spring	Island Sun, Mar 27, 2009
Equine Couple	Island Sun, March 5, 2010
Mother	Island Sun, March 5, 2010
The Back Nine	Human Touch, Vol. 9, 2016
Ordinary	Human Touch, Vol. 9, 2016
Kisses at the Airport	Human Touch, Vol. 10, 2017
Just Words	Human Touch, Vol. 11, 2018
In the End, Beauty (now retitled "Beauty")	Human Touch, Vol. 11, 2018
Tears	Human Touch, Vol. 11, 2018
The Task	Human Touch, Vol. 12, 2019
Love	Human Touch, Vol. 12, 2019
Raincloud	Human Touch, Vol. 12, 2019; Colorado Country March 5, 1019

ABOUT THE AUTHOR

Carol Ehrlich is a 93 year-old widow with a large, active family—19 directly related, plus 5 in-laws—who have watched and shared her exploits, her strains and pains, and her joys all these years. Her clinical career in audiology and speech pathology was spent at Children's Hospital Colorado and at Columbia Presbyterian Medical Center in New York City (Director Emerita of both clinics); she was also Assistant Professor of Audiology at Columbia University and at the University of Denver. Retiring in 1984, she indulged her love of classical music and the English language, living richly with both. She lived in Denver for many years, and for over 36 years in three other places: Ft. Myers, Florida; Aspen, Colorado; and a cherished cabin in Grand Lake, Colorado, together with her husband, Max, and drew from her experiences the material in this and her previous poetry collection, Winds in My Sails.

She has written numerous research reports while engaged professionally, as well as All Kinds of Love: Experiencing Hospice with co-author, Carolyn Jaffe.

Printed in the United States
By Bookmasters